Knitting Journal

This journal belongs to :

....

....

....

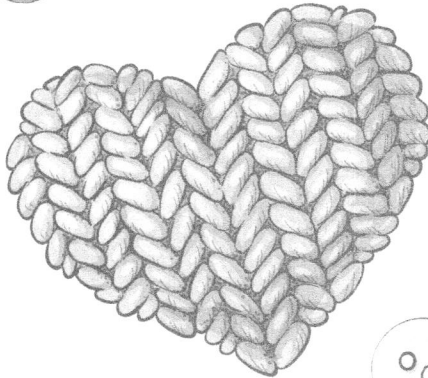

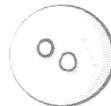

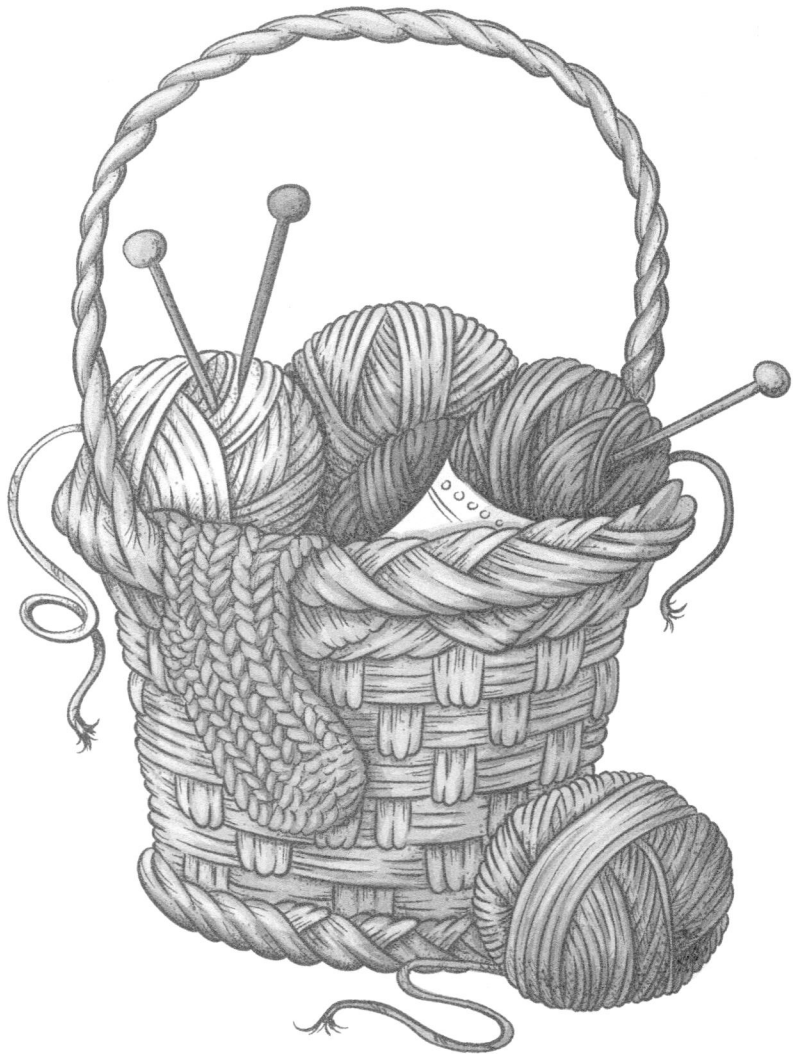

Index

Page	Name	For
6		
8		
10		
12		
14		
16		
18		
20		
22		
24		
26		
28		
30		
32		
34		
36		
38		
40		
42		
44		

Page	Name	For
46		
48		
50		
52		
54		
56		
58		
60		
62		
64		
66		
68		
70		
72		
74		
76		
78		
80		
82		
84		

Index

Page	Name	For
6		
8		
10		
12		
14		
16		
18		
20		
22		
24		
26		
28		
30		
32		
34		
36		
38		
40		
42		
44		

Page	Name	For
46		
48		
50		
52		
54		
56		
58		
60		
62		
64		
66		
68		
70		
72		
74		
76		
78		
80		
82		
84		

Page	Name	For
86		
88		
90		
92		
94		
96		
98		
100		
102		
104		
106		
108		
110		
112		
114		
116		
118		
120		
122		
124		

Project

Name : ....

For : ....

Occasion : ....

Start date : .... End date : ....

Type of Project : ....

Name of Pattern : ....

Sketch / Photo

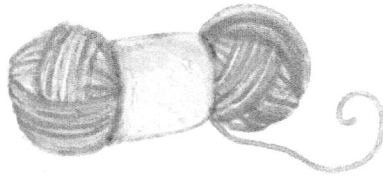

Yarn : ---

Fiber : --

Color / Dye lot : ---

Weight : ---------------------------------

Wpi : ---------------------------------------

Gauge : ---------------------------------

Needles : -------------------------------

Washing Instructions : ---

Notes : ---

Project

Name : ....

For : ....

Occasion : ....

Start date : .... End date : ....

Type of Project : ....

Name of Pattern : ....

Sketch / Photo

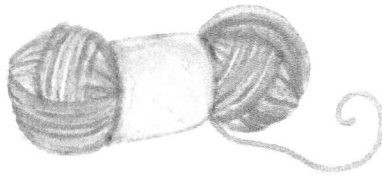

Yarn : ....

Fiber : ....

Color / Dye lot : ....

Weight : ....

Wpi : ....

Gauge : ....

Needles : ....

Sample

Washing Instructions : ....

....

Notes : ....

....

....

....

....

....

....

Project

Name : --

For : --

Occasion : --

Start date : ------------------- End date : -------------------

Type of Project : --

Name of Pattern : --

Sketch / Photo

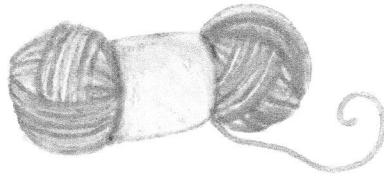

Yarn : --

Fiber : --

Color / Dye lot : --

Weight : -------------------------------------

Wpi : ---

Gauge : ---------------------------------------

Needles : -------------------------------------

Sample

Washing Instructions : ---

Notes : ---

Project

Name : ....

For : ....

Occasion : ....

Start date : .... End date : ....

Type of Project : ....

Name of Pattern : ....

Sketch / Photo

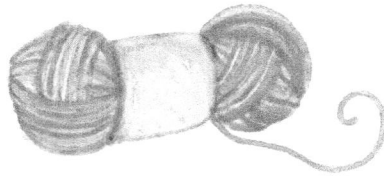

Yarn : --

Fiber : --

Color / Dye lot : ---

Weight : --------------------------------

Wpi : --------------------------------

Gauge : --------------------------------

Needles : -------------------------------

Sample

Washing Instructions : --

Notes : ---

Project

Name : ---

For : ---

Occasion : --

Start date : -------------------------- End date : ----------------

Type of Project : --

Name of Pattern : --

Sketch / Photo

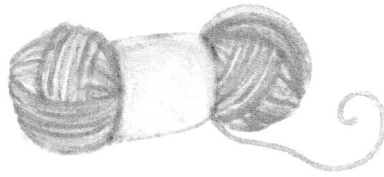

Yarn : ....

Fiber : ....

Color / Dye lot : ....

Weight : ....

Wpi : ....

Gauge : ....

Needles : ....

Sample

Washing Instructions : ....

....

Notes : ....

....

....

....

....

....

....

Project

Name : ....

For : ....

Occasion : ....

Start date : .... End date : ....

Type of Project : ....

Name of Pattern : ....

Sketch / Photo

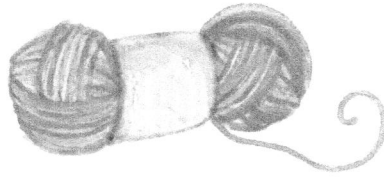

Yarn : --

Fiber : --

Color / Dye lot : --

Weight : ---------------------------------

Wpi : -------------------------------------

Gauge : ----------------------------------

Needles : --------------------------------

Sample

Washing Instructions : --

Notes : --

Project

Name : ....

For : ....

Occasion : ....

Start date : .... End date : ....

Type of Project : ....

Name of Pattern : ....

Sketch / Photo

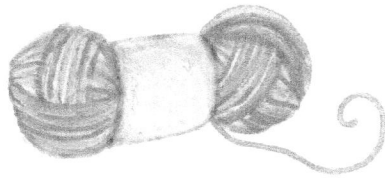

Yarn : ....

Fiber : ....

Color / Dye lot : ....

Weight : ....

Wpi : ....

Gauge : ....

Needles : ....

Sample

Washing Instructions : ....

....

Notes : ....

....

....

....

....

....

....

....

Project

Name : ....

For : ....

Occasion : ....

Start date : .... End date : ....

Type of Project : ....

Name of Pattern : ....

Sketch / Photo

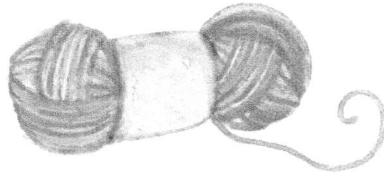

Yarn : --

Fiber : ---

Color / Dye lot : ---

Weight : --

Wpi : ---

Gauge : ---

Needles : --

Sample

Washing Instructions : --------------------------------------

----

Notes : ---

Project

Name : ....

For : ....

Occasion : ....

Start date : .... End date : ....

Type of Project : ....

Name of Pattern : ....

Sketch / Photo

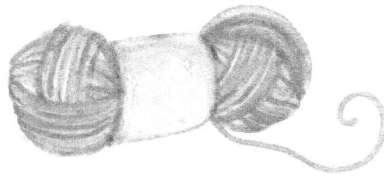

Yarn : -

Fiber : -

Color / Dye lot : -

Weight : -

Wpi : -

Gauge : -

Needles : -

Sample

Washing Instructions : -

- -

Notes : -

- -

- -

- -

- -

- -

- -

Project

Name : ....

For : ....

Occasion : ....

Start date : .... End date : ....

Type of Project : ....

Name of Pattern : ....

Sketch / Photo

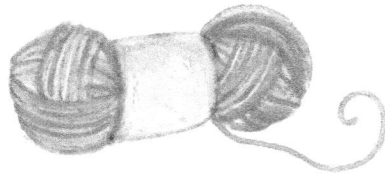

Yarn : ....

Fiber : ....

Color / Dye lot : ....

Weight : ....

Wpi : ....

Gauge : ....

Needles : ....

Sample

Washing Instructions : ....
....

Notes : ....
....
....
....
....
....
....
....

Project

Name : ....

For : ....

Occasion : ....

Start date : .... End date : ....

Type of Project : ....
Name of Pattern : ....

Sketch / Photo

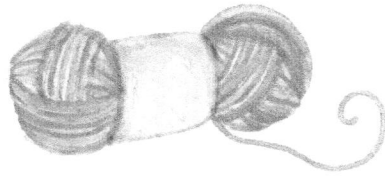

Yarn : --

Fiber : --

Color / Dye lot : --

Weight : --------------------------------

Wpi : ---------------------------------------

Gauge : -------------------------------

Needles : ------------------------------

Sample

Washing Instructions : ---

Notes : ---

Project

Name : ....

For : ....

Occasion : ....

Start date : .... End date : ....

Type of Project : ....

Name of Pattern : ....

Sketch / Photo

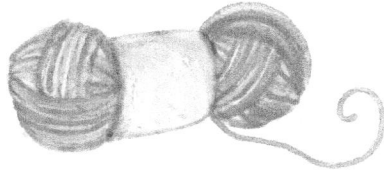

Yarn : --

Fiber : --

Color / Dye lot : --

Weight : ----------------------------------

Wpi : --

Gauge : --------------------------------------

Needles : ------------------------------------

Washing Instructions : ------------------------------------

Notes : --

Project

Name : ....

For : ....

Occasion : ....

Start date : .... End date : ....

Type of Project : ....

Name of Pattern : ....

Sketch / Photo

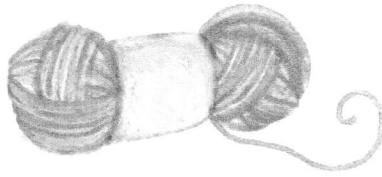

Yarn : ....

Fiber : ....

Color / Dye lot : ....

Weight : ....

Wpi : ....

Gauge : ....

Needles : ....

Sample

Washing Instructions : ....

....

Notes : ....

....

....

....

....

....

....

....

Project

Name : ....

For : ....

Occasion : ....

Start date : .... End date : ....

Type of Project : ....

Name of Pattern : ....

Sketch / Photo

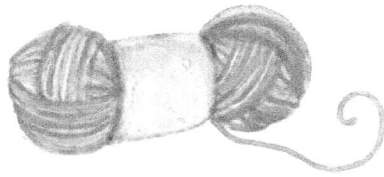

Yarn : --

Fiber : ---

Color / Dye lot : --

Weight : ----------------------------------

Wpi : ------------------------------------

Gauge : -----------------------------------

Needles : ----------------------------------

Sample

Washing Instructions : ---

Notes : ---

Project

Name : ....

For : ....

Occasion : ....

Start date : .... End date : ....

Type of Project : ....

Name of Pattern : ....

Sketch / Photo

Yarn : ....

Fiber : ....

Color / Dye lot : ....

Weight : ....

Wpi : ....

Gauge : ....

Needles : ....

Sample

Washing Instructions : ....

....

Notes : ....

....

....

....

....

....

....

Project

Name : ....

For : ....

Occasion : ....

Start date : .... End date : ....

Type of Project : ....

Name of Pattern : ....

Sketch / Photo

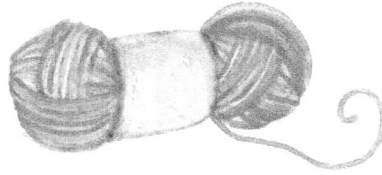

Yarn : ---

Fiber : ---

Color / Dye lot : ---------------------------------------

Weight : ------------------------------------

Wpi : ---------------------------------------

Gauge : ----------------------------------

Needles : --------------------------------

Sample

Washing Instructions : --------------------------------

Notes : --

Project

Name : ....

For : ....

Occasion : ....

Start date : .... End date : ....

Type of Project : ....

Name of Pattern : ....

Sketch / Photo

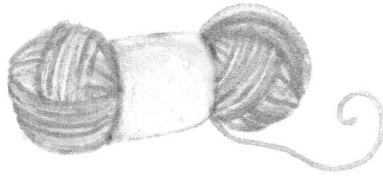

Yarn : --

Fiber : --

Color / Dye lot : ---

Weight : ----------------------------

Wpi : ----------------------------------

Gauge : ------------------------------

Needles : ----------------------------

Sample

Washing Instructions : ------------------------------------

Notes : ---

Project

Name : _____

For : _____

Occasion : _____

Start date : _____ End date : _____

Type of Project : _____

Name of Pattern : _____

Sketch / Photo

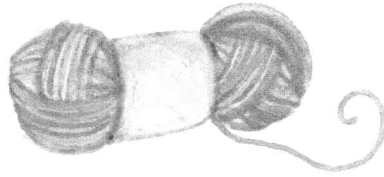

Yarn : _____

Fiber : _____

Color / Dye lot : _____

Weight : _____

Wpi : _____

Gauge : _____

Needles : _____

Sample

Washing Instructions : _____
_____

Notes : _____
_____
_____
_____
_____
_____
_____

Project

Name : --

For : --

Occasion : ---

Start date : ------------------------ End date : ------------------------

Type of Project : ---

Name of Pattern : ---

Sketch / Photo

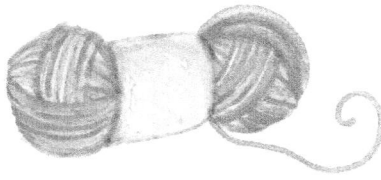

Yarn : ....

Fiber : ....

Color / Dye lot : ....

Weight : ....

Wpi : ....

Gauge : ....

Needles : ....

Sample

Washing Instructions : ....

....

Notes : ....

....

....

....

....

....

....

Project

Name : ....

For : ....

Occasion : ....

Start date : .... End date : ....

Type of Project : ....

Name of Pattern : ....

Sketch / Photo

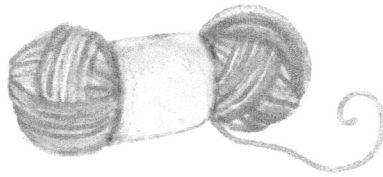

Yarn : ....

Fiber : ....

Color / Dye lot : ....

Weight : ....

Wpi : ....

Gauge : ....

Needles : ....

Sample

Washing Instructions : ....

....

Notes : ....

....

....

....

....

....

....

Project

Name : --

For : --

Occasion : --

Start date : ------------------------ End date : ---------------------------

Type of Project : ---

Name of Pattern : --

Sketch / Photo

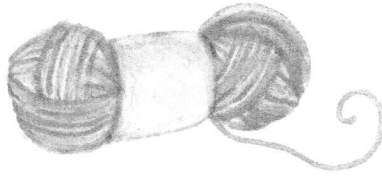

Yarn : ....

Fiber : ....

Color / Dye lot : ....

Weight : ....

Wpi : ....

Gauge : ....

Needles : ....

Washing Instructions : ....

....

Notes : ....

....

....

....

....

....

....

Project

Name : ....

For : ....

Occasion : ....

Start date : .... End date : ....

Type of Project : ....

Name of Pattern : ....

Sketch / Photo

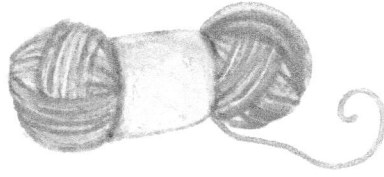

Yarn : --

Fiber : --

Color / Dye lot : --

Weight : -----------------------------------

Wpi : -----------------------------------

Gauge : -----------------------------------

Needles : ---------------------------------

Sample

Washing Instructions : --

Notes : --

Project

Name : ....

For : ....

Occasion : ....

Start date : .... End date : ....

Type of Project : ....

Name of Pattern : ....

Sketch / Photo

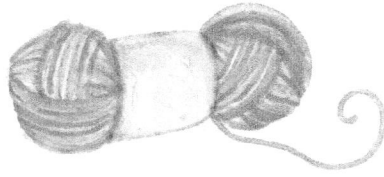

Yarn : ....

Fiber : ....

Color / Dye lot : ....

Weight : ....

Wpi : ....

Gauge : ....

Needles : ....

Sample

Washing Instructions : ....

....

Notes : ....

....

....

....

....

....

....

Project

Name : ....

For : ....

Occasion : ....

Start date : .... End date : ....

Type of Project : ....

Name of Pattern : ....

Sketch / Photo

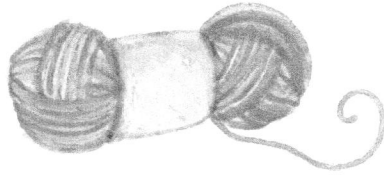

Yarn : --

Fiber : ---

Color / Dye lot : --

Weight : ---

Wpi : --

Gauge : --

Needles : --

Sample

Washing Instructions : -----------------------------------

Notes : ---

Project

Name : ....

For : ....

Occasion : ....

Start date : .... End date : ....

Type of Project : ....

Name of Pattern : ....

Sketch / Photo

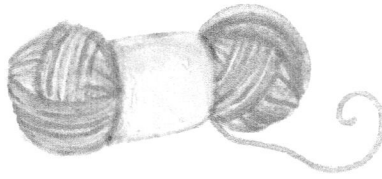

Yarn : --

Fiber : ---

Color / Dye lot : ---

Weight : -----------------------------------

Wpi : --------------------------------------

Gauge : ------------------------------------

Needles : ----------------------------------

Sample

Washing Instructions : --

Notes : ---

Project

Name : ....

For : ....

Occasion : ....

Start date : .... End date : ....

Type of Project : ....

Name of Pattern : ....

Sketch / Photo

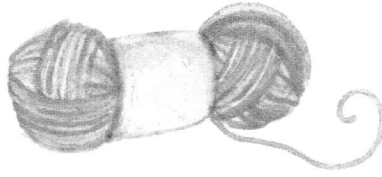

Yarn : --

Fiber : ---

Color / Dye lot : ---

Weight : ---------------------------------

Wpi : ---------------------------------------

Gauge : ------------------------------------

Needles : ---------------------------------

Sample

Washing Instructions : ---------------------------------

Notes : --

Project

Name : ....

For : ....

Occasion : ....

Start date : .... End date : ....

Type of Project : ....

Name of Pattern : ....

Sketch / Photo

Yarn : ....

Fiber : ....

Color / Dye lot : ....

Weight : ....

Wpi : ....

Gauge : ....

Needles : ....

Sample

Washing Instructions : ....

....

Notes : ....

....

....

....

....

....

....

Project

Name : ....

For : ....

Occasion : ....

Start date : .... End date : ....

Type of Project : ....

Name of Pattern : ....

Sketch / Photo

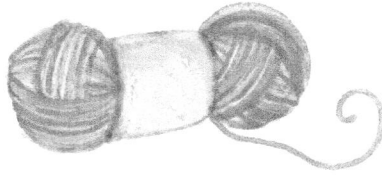

Yarn : --

Fiber : --

Color / Dye lot : --

Weight : --

Wpi : ---

Gauge : --

Needles : ---------------------------------------

Sample

Washing Instructions : ---

Notes : ---

Project

Name : ....

For : ....

Occasion : ....

Start date : .... End date : ....

Type of Project : ....

Name of Pattern : ....

Sketch / Photo

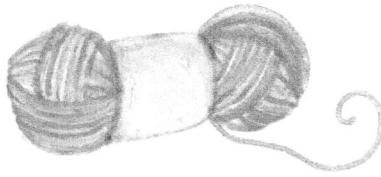

Yarn : --

Fiber : ---

Color / Dye lot : ---

Weight : ---

Wpi : ---

Gauge : --

Needles : --

Sample

Washing Instructions : ---

Notes : ---

Project

Name : ....

For : ....

Occasion : ....

Start date : .... End date : ....

Type of Project : ....

Name of Pattern : ....

Sketch / Photo

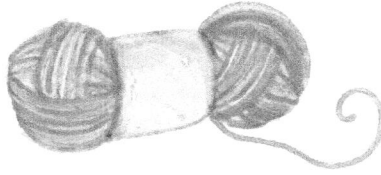

Yarn : ....

Fiber : ....

Color / Dye lot : ....

Weight : ....

Wpi : ....

Gauge : ....

Needles : ....

Sample

Washing Instructions : ....

....

Notes : ....

....

....

....

....

....

....

Project

Name : ....

For : ....

Occasion : ....

Start date : .... End date : ....

Type of Project : ....

Name of Pattern : ....

Sketch / Photo

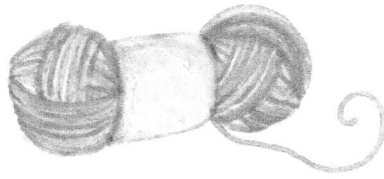

Yarn : ....

Fiber : ....

Color / Dye lot : ....

Weight : ....

Wpi : ....

Gauge : ....

Needles : ....

Sample

Washing Instructions : ....

....

Notes : ....

....

....

....

....

....

Project

Name : ....

For : ....

Occasion : ....

Start date : .... End date : ....

Type of Project : ....

Name of Pattern : ....

Sketch / Photo

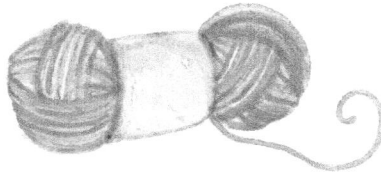

Yarn : ---

Fiber : --

Color / Dye lot : --

Weight : -------------------------------

Wpi : ----------------------------------

Gauge : --------------------------------

Needles : ------------------------------

Washing Instructions : ---

Notes : --

Project

Name : ....

For : ....

Occasion : ....

Start date : .... End date : ....

Type of Project : ....

Name of Pattern : ....

Sketch / Photo

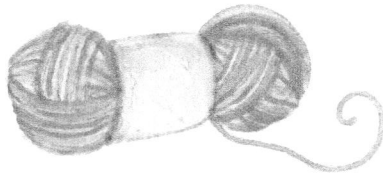

Yarn : ....

Fiber : ....

Color / Dye lot : ....

Weight : ....

Wpi : ....

Gauge : ....

Needles : ....

Washing Instructions : ....

....

Notes : ....

....

....

....

....

....

....

Sample

Project

Name : ....

For : ....

Occasion : ....

Start date : .... End date : ....

Type of Project : ....

Name of Pattern : ....

Sketch / Photo

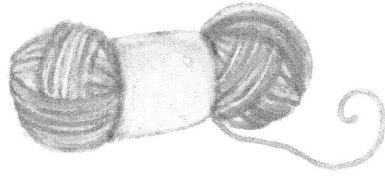

Yarn : ---

Fiber : ---

Color / Dye lot : --

Weight : -----------------------------------

Wpi : ---------------------------------------

Gauge : -------------------------------------

Needles : -----------------------------------

Sample

Washing Instructions : ---

Notes : ---

Project

Name : --

For : ---

Occasion : ---

Start date : ---------------------- End date : ------------------------

Type of Project : ---

Name of Pattern : ---

Sketch / Photo

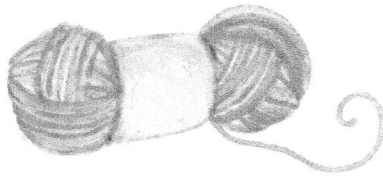

Yarn : --

Fiber : --

Color / Dye lot : --

Weight : --

Wpi : --

Gauge : --

Needles : --

Sample

Washing Instructions : --

Notes : --

Project

Name : --

For : --

Occasion : --

Start date : -------------------- End date : ------------------

Type of Project : --

Name of Pattern : --

Sketch / Photo

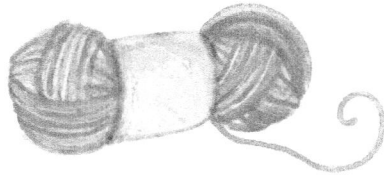

Yarn : ....

Fiber : ....

Color / Dye lot : ....

Weight : ....

Wpi : ....

Gauge : ....

Needles : ....

Sample

Washing Instructions : ....

....

Notes : ....

....

....

....

....

....

....

Project

Name : --

For : --

Occasion : --

Start date : ------------------------ End date : ----------------------

Type of Project : ---
Name of Pattern : ---

Sketch / Photo

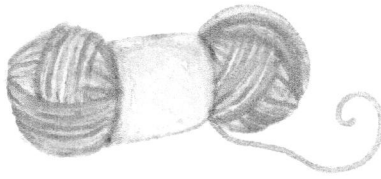

Yarn : --

Fiber : ---

Color / Dye lot : --

Weight : ------------------------------

Wpi : -----------------------------------

Gauge : ---------------------------------

Needles : -------------------------------

Sample

Washing Instructions : -----------------------------

Notes : ---

Project

Name : ....

For : ....

Occasion : ....

Start date : .... End date : ....

Type of Project : ....
Name of Pattern : ....

Sketch / Photo

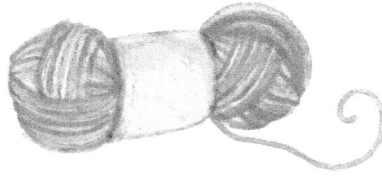

Yarn : --

Fiber : --

Color / Dye lot : --

Weight : --------------------------------

Wpi : --------------------------------

Gauge : --------------------------------

Needles : --------------------------------

Sample

Washing Instructions : ---

Notes : --

Project

Name : --

For : ---

Occasion : --

Start date : ------------------- End date : ------------------------

Type of Project : ---

Name of Pattern : --

Sketch / Photo

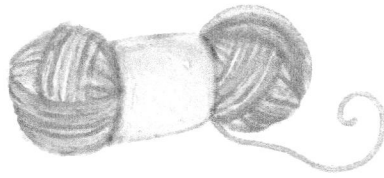

Yarn : --

Fiber : ---

Color / Dye lot : ---

Weight : ----------------------------

Wpi : --------------------------------

Gauge : -----------------------------

Needles : ---------------------------

Sample

Washing Instructions : ---

Notes : ---

Project

Name : ....

For : ....

Occasion : ....

Start date : .... End date : ....

Type of Project : ....

Name of Pattern : ....

Sketch / Photo

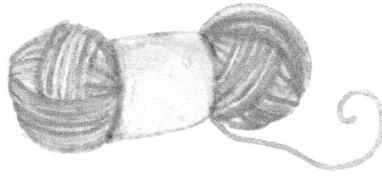

Yarn : ....

Fiber : ....

Color / Dye lot : ....

Weight : ....

Wpi : ....

Gauge : ....

Needles : ....

Sample

Washing Instructions : ....

....

Notes : ....

....

....

....

....

....

....

Project

Name : --

For : --

Occasion : --

Start date : ------------------- End date : ---------------

Type of Project : ---

Name of Pattern : ---

Sketch / Photo

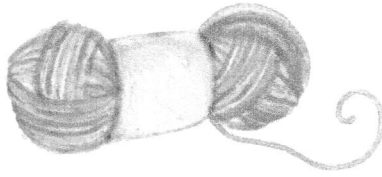

Yarn : ....

Fiber : ....

Color / Dye lot : ....

Weight : ....

Wpi : ....

Gauge : ....

Needles : ....

Sample

Washing Instructions : ....

....

Notes : ....

....

....

....

....

....

....

Project

Name : ....

For : ....

Occasion : ....

Start date : .... End date : ....

Type of Project : ....

Name of Pattern : ....

Sketch / Photo

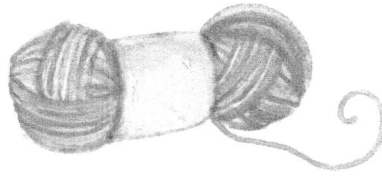

Yarn : ....

Fiber : ....

Color / Dye lot : ....

Weight : ....

Wpi : ....

Gauge : ....

Needles : ....

Sample

Washing Instructions : ....
....

Notes : ....
....
....
....
....
....
....
....

Project

Name : --

For : --

Occasion : --

Start date : ----------------------- End date : ----------------

Type of Project : ---

Name of Pattern : ---

Sketch / Photo

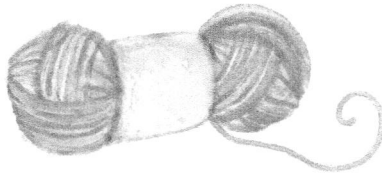

Yarn : ....

Fiber : ....

Color / Dye lot : ....

Weight : ....

Wpi : ....

Gauge : ....

Needles : ....

Sample

Washing Instructions : ....
....

Notes : ....
....
....
....
....
....
....

Project

Name : ....

For : ....

Occasion : ....

Start date : .... End date : ....

Type of Project : ....

Name of Pattern : ....

Sketch / Photo

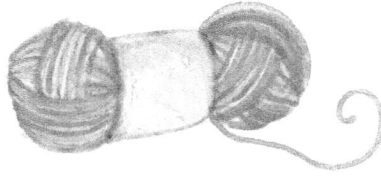

Yarn : ....

Fiber : ....

Color / Dye lot : ....

Weight : ....

Wpi : ....

Gauge : ....

Needles : ....

Sample

Washing Instructions : ....

....

Notes : ....

....

....

....

....

....

....

Project

Name : --

For : --

Occasion : --

Start date : ------------------------------ End date : ---------------------

Type of Project : --

Name of Pattern : --

Sketch / Photo

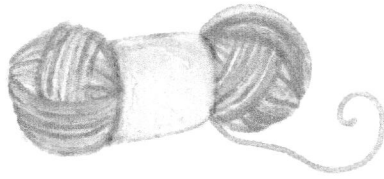

Yarn : ....

Fiber : ....

Color / Dye lot : ....

Weight : ....

Wpi : ....

Gauge : ....

Needles : ....

Washing Instructions : ....

....

Notes : ....

....

....

....

....

....

....

Project

Name : --

For : --

Occasion : --

Start date : --------------------- End date : ------------------------

Type of Project : --

Name of Pattern : --

Sketch / Photo

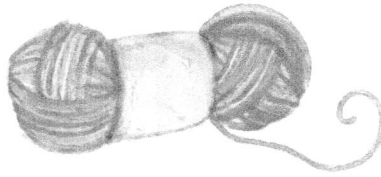

Yarn :

Fiber :

Color / Dye lot :

Weight :

Wpi :

Gauge :

Needles :

Sample

Washing Instructions :

Notes :

Project

Name : --

For : --

Occasion : --

Start date : ------------------------ End date : ----------------------------------

Type of Project : --

Name of Pattern : --

Sketch / Photo

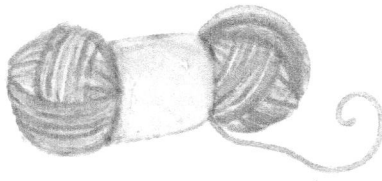

Yarn : ....

Fiber : ....

Color / Dye lot : ....

Weight : ....

Wpi : ....

Gauge : ....

Needles : ....

Sample

Washing Instructions : ....

....

Notes : ....

....

....

....

....

....

....

Project

Name : ....

For : ....

Occasion : ....

Start date : .... End date : ....

Type of Project : ....

Name of Pattern : ....

Sketch / Photo

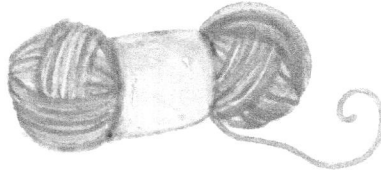

Yarn : --

Fiber : --

Color / Dye lot : --------------------------------

Weight : -------------------------

Wpi : -------------------------

Gauge : -------------------------

Needles : -------------------------

Sample

Washing Instructions : --------------------------

Notes : --

Project

Name : ....

For : ....

Occasion : ....

Start date : .... End date : ....

Type of Project : ....

Name of Pattern : ....

Sketch / Photo

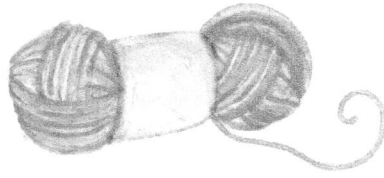

Yarn : --

Fiber : --

Color / Dye lot : --

Weight : ----------------------------

Wpi : -----------------------------------

Gauge : -----------------------------

Needles : --------------------------

Sample

Washing Instructions : --------------------------------------

----

Notes : ---

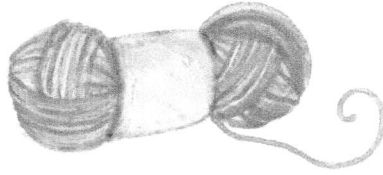

Yarn : ....

Fiber : ....

Color / Dye lot : ....

Weight : ....

Wpi : ....

Gauge : ....

Needles : ....

Sample

Washing Instructions : ....

....

Notes : ....

....

....

....

....

....

....

Project

Name : ....

For : ....

Occasion : ....

Start date : .... End date : ....

Type of Project : ....

Name of Pattern : ....

Sketch / Photo

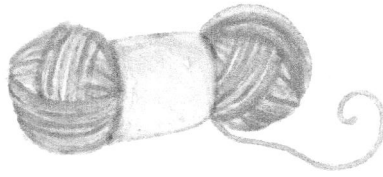

Yarn : ....

Fiber : ....

Color / Dye lot : ....

Weight : ....

Wpi : ....

Gauge : ....

Needles : ....

Washing Instructions : ....

....

Notes : ....

....

....

....

....

....

....

Project

Name : ....

For : ....

Occasion : ....

Start date : .... End date : ....

Type of Project : ....

Name of Pattern : ....

Sketch / Photo

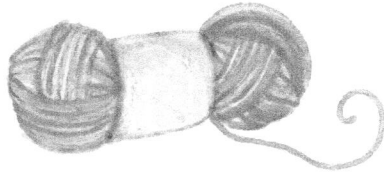

Yarn : --

Fiber : --

Color / Dye lot : ---------------------------

Weight : ------------------------

Wpi : -------------------------------

Gauge : ----------------------

Needles : --------------------

Sample

Washing Instructions : -------------------------

Notes : --

Project

Name : ---

For : --

Occasion : --

Start date : ------------------ End date : ---------------

Type of Project : ---------------------------------------

Name of Pattern : ---------------------------------------

Sketch / Photo

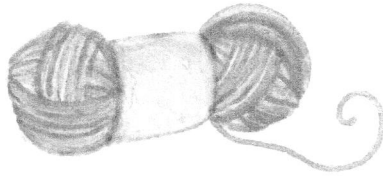

Yarn : --

Fiber : ---

Color / Dye lot : --

Weight : ----------------------------------

Wpi : -------------------------------------

Gauge : -----------------------------------

Needles : ---------------------------------

Sample

Washing Instructions : ---

Notes : ---

Project

Name : ....

For : ....

Occasion : ....

Start date : .... End date : ....

Type of Project : ....

Name of Pattern : ....

Sketch / Photo

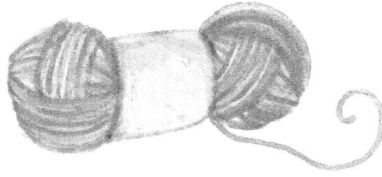

Yarn : ....

Fiber : ....

Color / Dye lot : ....

Weight : ....

Wpi : ....

Gauge : ....

Needles : ....

Sample

Washing Instructions : ....

....

Notes : ....

....

....

....

....

....

....

Project

Name : ....

For : ....

Occasion : ....

Start date : .... End date : ....

Type of Project : ....

Name of Pattern : ....

Sketch / Photo

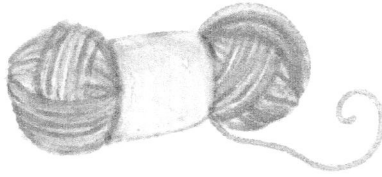

Yarn : --

Fiber : ---

Color / Dye lot : ---

Weight : -------------------------

Wpi : -------------------------

Gauge : -----------------------

Needles : ---------------------

Sample

Washing Instructions : --

Notes : ---

Project

Name : ....

For : ....

Occasion : ....

Start date : .... End date : ....

Type of Project : ....

Name of Pattern : ....

Sketch / Photo

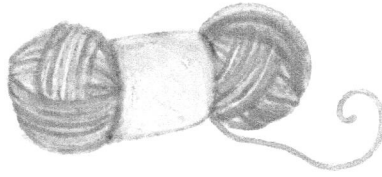

Yarn : ....

Fiber : ....

Color / Dye lot : ....

Weight : ....

Wpi : ....

Gauge : ....

Needles : ....

Sample

Washing Instructions : ....

....

Notes : ....

....

....

....

....

....

....

Project

Name : --

For : ---

Occasion : --

Start date : ------------------- End date : ------------------------

Type of Project : ---

Name of Pattern : ---

Sketch / Photo

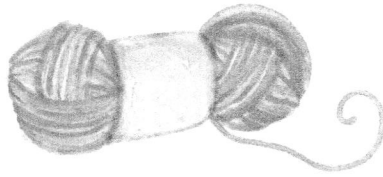

Yarn : ....

Fiber : ....

Color / Dye lot : ....

Weight : ....

Wpi : ....

Gauge : ....

Needles : ....

Sample

Washing Instructions : ....

....

Notes : ....

....

....

....

....

....

....

Project

Name : ....

For : ....

Occasion : ....

Start date : .... End date : ....

Type of Project : ....

Name of Pattern : ....

Sketch / Photo

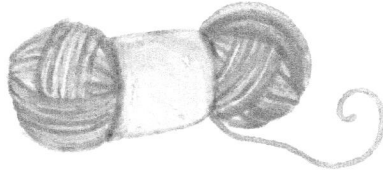

Yarn : _____

Fiber : _____

Color / Dye lot : _____

Weight : _____

Wpi : _____

Gauge : _____

Needles : _____

Sample

Washing Instructions : _____

_____

Notes : _____

_____

_____

_____

_____

_____

_____

Project

Name : -

For : -

Occasion : -

Start date : - - - - - - - - - - - - - - - End date : - - - - - - - - - - - -

Type of Project : -

Name of Pattern : -

Sketch / Photo

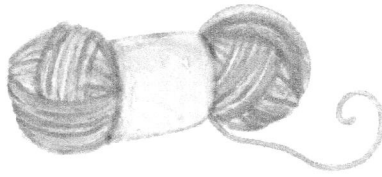

Yarn : ....

Fiber : ....

Color / Dye lot : ....

Weight : ....

Wpi : ....

Gauge : ....

Needles : ....

```
Sample
```

Washing Instructions : ....

....

Notes : ....

....

....

....

....

....

....

Project

Name : ....

For : ....

Occasion : ....

Start date : .... End date : ....

Type of Project : ....

Name of Pattern : ....

Sketch / Photo

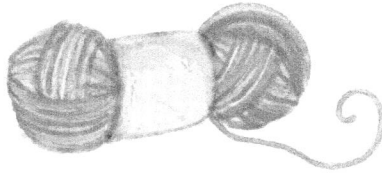

Yarn : ....

Fiber : ....

Color / Dye lot : ....

Weight : ....

Wpi : ....

Gauge : ....

Needles : ....

Sample

Washing Instructions : ....

....

Notes : ....

....

....

....

....

....

....

....

Project

Name : --

For : ---

Occasion : --

Start date : ------------------- End date : -------------------------

Type of Project : ---

Name of Pattern : ---

Sketch / Photo

Yarn :

Fiber :

Color / Dye lot :

Weight :

Wpi :

Gauge :

Needles :

Sample

Washing Instructions :

Notes :

Made in the USA
Monee, IL
19 January 2022